NICE

Photos by Heli Flach

Editions KINA ITALIA

The city, famous for its Carnival, its festival of flowers and its artistic monuments, as well as for the beauty of its location and its climate, is located in an area which was already inhabited by humans over 400,000 years ago.

Around the 4th century B.C. the Greek colonists of Focea occupied the site, which they called Nikaia, and were later succeeded by peoples of Ligurian origin.

Two centuries later the Romans arrived and founded a town (Cemenelum) on the hill of Cimiez, which quickly became the most important military and administrative center in the region, overwhelming the Greek Nikaia.

It was not until the 10th century, after the end of the nightmare of barbarian and Saracen devastation that had caused irreparable damage to Cemenelum in particular, did Nice, an episcopal seat since the 5th century, reassume a preeminent position, placing itself under the protection of the Count of Provence.

But the city's desire for independence, which had manifested as early as the 12th century, inspired it to abandon the Provençal dynasty in 1388 and to voluntarily place itself

1) The Promenade des Anglais.
2) Hotel Elisée Palace.

2

1

2

under the control of Count Amadeus VII of Savoy. Nice remained tied to the House of Savoy almost until 1860, with shifting fortunes.

The abrupt disownment had its consequences, and during the 16th century the city was assaulted time and time again by French and Turkish troops, although each time it managed to withstand the attacks.

Having overcome these assaults, the fortress of Nice (fortified in the 16th century) was nevertheless razed to the ground by the French in 1706.

Favored by Napoleon, who stayed here for long periods after 1792, the year in which the city requested to be annexed to France, Nice (where Giuseppe Garibaldi was born in 1807) returned to the Savoys in 1814, and only the referendum of 1860 sanctioned its permanent transfer to France.

From this time on the "queen of the Riviera," frequented primarily by the English since the late 18th century, experienced a surprising spate of development, both in economic terms and with the construction of large hotels, elegant villas and luxurious buildings.

The "golden age" of tourism in Nice had begun, and continues to this day. If a visit to Nice must of necessity include a walk along the splendid Promenade des Anglais, the museums and monuments of this city of a thousand surprises are also a must.

Those who prefer a cultural visit can choose between the Musée Terra Amata, the Musée Masséna, dedicated to the history and art of the city, the Musée des Beaux-Arts, with its antique and contemporary collections, the Musée d'Art Naïf, the Musée Naval, the Musée d'Art Moderne et Contemporain, the Musée d'Histoire Naturelle, or, at Cimiez, the prestigious Marc Chagall and Matisse museums and the lavish Musée d'Archéologie.

Art and architecture soar to their greatest heights in the city, both in the streets and the beautiful squares crowned by buildings, and in the monuments, for example the church

1

1) The Promenade des Anglais and the Plage des Ponchettes.
2) The Espace Massena fountains.

of Saints Martin and Augustin, the oldest parish in Nice (16th century), the baroque cathedral of Sainte-Réparate, and the 17th century churches of Saint-Jacques and Saint-Guillaume.

Baroque style triumphs in the luxurious Lascaris palace with its elegant monumental staircase, in the refined chapels of the Pénitents Blancs and the Pénitents Noirs, and in the marvelous Chapelle de l'Annonciation. The old Franciscan monastery (15th-17th centuries) erected on the hill of Cimiez, with its splendid Gothic church of Notre-Dame-de-l'Assomption, is the sites of greatest interest in this part of the city, along with the remains of Roman times (thermal baths from the 3rd century B.C., amphitheaters, an early Christian baptistry, parts of the original oppidum and several necropolises).

THE HÔTEL NEGRESCO

The renowned Promenade des Anglais, which curves along the Bay of Angels (Baie des Anges), owes its fame not only to the spectacular view of the sea and the stretch of coast from the Nice promontory to Fort Carré in Antibes, but also to the opulent, elegant architecture of the numerous palaces that line it. Some of the splendid examples of late 19th century and early 20th century architecture along the Promenade include the Hôtel Negresco, built during the Belle Époque according to the most classical rules of baroque style.

Henry Negresco, a musician of gypsy origin who emigrated to France from Romania in the early 20th century, was responsible for its construction. Negresco decided to build his palace in the most elegant, renowned area of the city at that time, the route the English had built in the 19th century that had quickly become a meeting place for the high society that frequented Nice. To build it, he relied on the creative genius of the French architect Edouard Niermans, who was responsible for famous projects like the Casino and the Moulin Rouge building in Paris.

1) The Promenade des Anglais and the Hotel Negresco at night.
2) Hall within the Hotel Negresco.

Niermans did not disappoint his client, and created a spectacular palace that blended baroque harmony and splendor, a grandiose structure and elegant details, abundant ornamentation and the most refined sophistication. Completed in 1912, the Hôtel soon became one of the most prestigious and elegant places in the city, and immediately attracted a clientèle that included aristocrats and wealthy bourgeoisie, who found at the Negresco an atmosphere and surroundings worthy of the most luxurious royal or imperial palaces of Europe.

When World War I exploded, the Hôtel Negresco suffered a difficult, tormented period. The building was in fact requisitioned and transformed into a military hospital. The precious furnishings of the palace's splendid salons and rooms, which until then had received a very different segment of humanity, suffered serious damage that could not be remedied after the war, for reasons that included the death of Henry Negresco. With damage so grave that it was threatened with demolition, in the late 1950's the building was bought by the Auger family, who decided to restore the Hôtel Negresco to its original splendor.

Inside the Hôtel Negresco:
1) The Salon Royal.
2) Room 122.
3) The Salon Louis XIV.
4) The bar.

THE HÔTEL NEGRESCO

Today, thanks to their dedication, the palace (a French national monument since 1974), with its majestic façade dominated by the great rose-colored cupola, has rooms adorned with refined materials and precious furnishings, true works of art like 17th century tapestries and paintings, masterpieces by Picasso and Dufy, and priceless carpets that offer today's visitors the sophisticated atmosphere of the turn-of-the-century Negresco. The guest rooms, each one furnished in a different style, have welcomed famous persons like English royalty, Winston Churchill, Charlie Chaplin and numerous other artists, international personalities and show business celebrities.

1-2-3-4) Views of the Promenade des Anglais, the beaches and the Hôtel Negresco.
5) The Casino RUHL.

4

5

1

RUE PIÉTONNE

This name is traditionally used to indicate the downtown area of the city closed to automobile traffic, and is delimited by the rue de France and rue Masséna. Along these lovely streets lined with elegant 19th century buildings and crowded with people at every hour of the day, there are numerous shops, stores, restaurants and cafes that have become famous meeting places in the city. In the immediate vicinity is the Place et Espace Masséna (named after the famous Nice marshal), set off by the beautiful architecture of the Italian-style palazzi built in the early 19th century and the fountain adorned by bronze horses. Another elegant fountain decorates the nearby Albert I Gardens, which are located near the seaside promenade.

1

2

1-2) Views of the Rue piétonne.
3) The painter Jean Louis CARINA before one of his works.

Of extremely ancient origins, the Carnival of Nice is one of the liveliest and most spectacular in Europe. From medieval times to the late 18th century, the festival took place solely in the city's old quarter, at the end of Lent. Suspended during the French Revolution, the Carnival re-commenced only in 1830, to celebrate the city's return to Savoy domination, ratified in the Treaty of Paris. In its present form, with a set route and a different theme each year, the Carnival of Nice hearkens back to the tradition established in 1873. It opens three weeks before Mardi Gras with the entry of the Carnival King, followed by festive parades of allegorical theme floats, surrounded by crowds of costumed merry-makers.

A float.

THE BATTLE OF FLOWERS

This characteristic event, which is also a part of the great Carnival festivities, has an alter ego in the Italian Battle of Oranges at Ivrea, although it is certainly more picturesque and less bloody! On Wednesday, along streets crowded with costumed merry-makers, some wearing typical large caricatured heads of papier-mâché, the pride of local artisans, thousands of people watch or participate in this cheerful, colorful battle with multihued petals that replace confetti for a day. The millions of flowers used, most of them cultivated in the region's nurseries, paint the sky and streets of Nice with color, almost as if anticipating the arrival of spring.

The battle of flowers.

Built by the architect Lenormand in imitation of the great French early Gothic cathedrals (Notre-Dame of Paris and the cathedral in Leon), this church has elegant Gothic lines made slightly heavier by the bulk and modest height of the majestic edifice. The façade, preceded by a short stairway, is divided into three horizontal orders. The first order has an elegant central portal, flanked by two smaller portals, both splayed. The second order, with the great central rose window, is flanked by two mullioned windows with two lights, above the side portals. The third order, including the cornice with mullioned blind windows, is dominated by two square towers standing at the side portals.

1) Celebrating Mass.
2) The façade of the Notre-Dame Cathedral.

2

1

A majestic testimony to the presence of an important community of Russian families along the Côte d'Azur, particularly in Nice, until the end of the 18th century, this Orthodox cathedral brightens the city skyline with its elegant forms and precious decorations. It is one of the largest Russian Orthodox churches ever built outside Russia. Designed by the architect Préobrajensky on the site of the earlier Bermond villa, which was passed down to the imperial house of Romanov in the early 20th century, the cathedral was desired by numerous members of the Russian aristocracy who frequented the Côte d'Azur and wanted a place where they could gather for religious worship.

The rich exterior, decorated in colors of ochre, blue and gold, dominated by the characteristic six cupolas covered with glazed tiles surmounted by crosses and elegant mosaics on the façade, matches the magnificence of the interior, with a Greek cross floor plan centered on the marvelous iconostasis similar to that of St. Basil's Cathedral in Moscow. The area is embellished with vaults covered in gold leaf, and splendid works of art adorn it, including icons, frescoes, and wood carvings. Of particular artistic value is

the wood table with the icon of the Madonna of Kazan, embellished with refined engravings of silver and precious stones. The entire imperial Russian family was present during the cathedral's opening ceremony in 1912.

1) The iconostatis.
2) Wood painting with the icon of the Madonna of Kazan.
3) The façade of the St. Nicholas Cathedral.

3

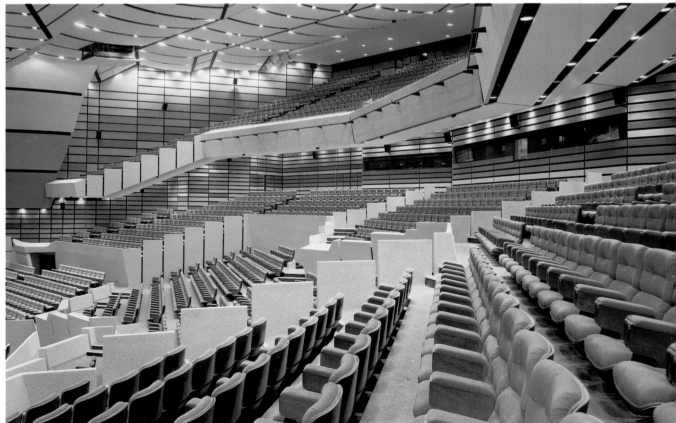

ACROPOLIS

This ultra-modern complex was designed in the mid-1980's by a group of Nice architects who took their inspiration from the form of a gigantic sailing ship "anchored" to the Paillon by five enormous vaults. Over 300 meters long, this grandiose structure, which houses the Palais des Arts, du Tourisme et des Congrès, is divided into various areas, which the architects named based on ancient Greek tradition. The agora, the spectacular entrance hall where the crystalline surfaces of the windows offset the metallic structure of the enormous sliding roof, is crowned by five floors that include conference areas, meeting rooms, radio-television production facilities and concert halls.

1-3) The Acropolis.
2) Overall view of the Auditorium Apollon.

3

MUSÉE MASSÉNA

This museum, which stands on the Promenade des Anglais and is surrounded by gardens, was built in the late 19th century for a descendant of the famous marshal of Nice. Inspired by the architecture of Italian villas of the period, the palazzo contains two floors of precious works of art depicting a number of subjects by various artists. The series of paintings and statues dedicated to the imperial house and family of Masséna (including a bust of the marshal done by Canova) are followed by works by primitive Nice and Italian artists, including a priceless silver reliquary from Renaissance Italy, the collection of 5th-17th century religious art and the assortment of weapons and armor, with rare ancient pieces.
One section of the museum is dedicated to the history of Nice.

MUSÉE D'ART MODERNE ET CONTEMPORAIN

Of certain interest for lovers of modern and contemporary art, this futuristic museum designed by architects Bayard and Vidal, displays numerous works of avant-garde French and American art from the 1960's to the present, from the Pop Art of Andy Warhol and George Segal to the Fluxus movement of John Cage, to the Nouveau Réalisme of Yves Klein (to whom an entire section is devoted), Arman and Christo, to minimalism and the most modern trends of the 20th century, with particular attention to the work of artists from the Nice school.
Extremely effective are the two grandiose works displayed outside the museum - a sculpture by Calder on the square and Klein's Wall of Fire on one of the terraces.

1) Façade of the Masséna Museum.
2) Museum of Modern and Contemporary Art.

THE FISH MARKET

The fish market is held between 7:00 am and lunch time every day except Monday, around the fountain at Place St-François. Here are stands of fresh seafood, which the fish vendors proclaim loudly, often in the colorful expressions of nissart, the dialect spoken in Nice. It's one of the most typical, animated spectacles in the city's tradition.

Photo on page 24-25:
Panorama of Nice.

Page 26
1-2) The fish market.
3) The fountain with dolphins.

2

1

Nice offers typical products, especially agricultural and farm goods from the region. Thus, in addition to the local wines (Château de Bellet) and olive oil, there are perfumes and essences prepared with herbs and flowers (Eau de Nice). There are also typical Provençal fabrics and the classic articles of regional craftspeople (glassware, china and earthenware).

1) Stuffing Nice-style.
2) Vegetables from the region.
3) Regional produce.
4) Fried food.
5) Fruit from the region.
6) The "socca".
7) Olives from Nice.
8) Swiss chard pastry.

1

3

2

4

5

1) View of Old Nice.
2) False Door.
3) The bustle of Old Nice.
4) Residence in the heart of Old Nice.
5) The Madonna of "Malonat".

THE FLOWER MARKET

Especially animated and picturesque, the traditional Nice flower market takes place every day except Monday, along the Cours Saleya near the beautiful Chapelle de la Miséricorde. From early in the morning to mid-afternoon, splendid flowers of every kind are displayed in the stands of this lively, colorful market.

1) The flower market.
2) The Chapelle de la Miséricorde.

Dating back to the second half of the 17th century, this edifice, designed by the local architect J.A. Guiberto, is consecrated to the martyred St. Réparate, the city's patron saint. A splendid example of the baroque style of Nice, the central portion of the cathedral, capped by the beautiful cupola covered with glazed tiles and adorned by the elegant decorated façade with the refined entry portal with its small arches, is accompanied by the bell tower, which came a century later but blends perfectly with the whole. The interior is grandiose, adorned by sumptuous friezes, marble work and elegant stucco work that provide harmonious examples of pure baroque art. The wood wainscoting that decorates the sacristy is also 17th century.

1) The cathedral façade.
2) View of the cathedral and the cupola, covered with glazed tiles.
3) The altar.

THE CASTLE

The hill where the castle once stood is one of the most scenic areas of the city. A walk up to the chateau provides a 360° view and allows the visitor to admire not only the entire topography of Nice, but also the surrounding hills. In close proximity to the city one can see the slopes of the hills covered with olive groves, which in their turn are crowned by the sea to the south, while to the east, west and north are highlands that soar up to become the higher Leuze and Agel mountain ranges, the Provençal mountains and the Alps. Following the splendid shaded walkway that leads to the terrace on top of the hill (which can also be reached by elevator), a few vestiges

1) The artificial waterfall.
2) The unusual little train that carries tourists to the castle.
3) The ruins within the castle: the rocks of ancient Nikaia.
4) The castle terraces.

2

3

of the city's ancient fortress are still visible. The defensive walls built on the hill prior to the 10th century were replaced in 1177 by a fortress built by the Marquis of Provence, Alfonse II. Destroyed and then rebuilt in the first half of the 13th century, the fortress, expanded in 1440, became a citadel in the early 16th century under Charles III of Savoy, who transferred the cathedral (there are still a few 11th century remains, beneath which ruins from the Greek and Roman eras have been discovered) to the church of Ste-Réparate. In 1543, after days of siege, the fortress was attacked by the Turks, who were unable to overcome it, due in part to the courage of one of the city's symbolic figures, Catherine Séguran. In 1560, Emanuel Filbert of Savoy repaired the damage the fortress suffered on this occasion, but in the late 17th century it was almost completely destroyed following an explosion of the powder magazine. The coup de grace for the chateau of Nice came from the cannon of Louis XIV, who razed it to the ground.

1) Ancient Nikaia.
2-3-4) Mosaic depicting the voyage of ULYSSES.

2

1

1) The Tour Bellanda.
2-4) Details of the Castle terrace.
3) View of the Promenade des Anglais from the Castle terrace.
5) The Castle as seen from the Promenade des Anglais.

5

THE PORT

For centuries, from the time the first colony was founded where Nice is located today to the mid-18th century, there was no mooring place that could truly be called a port, and all vessels that approached the coast had to drop anchor in the stretch of sea that extends to the foot of the castle fortress. In 1750, for both economic and strategic reasons, Charles Emanuel III, the Duke of Savoy (at that time, and until 1860, Nice belonged to the House of Savoy) ordered the construction of a true port to the east of the castle hill and began building on the marshy land of Lympia. Over a century later, between 1870 and the early 20th cen-

Views of Lympia harbor.

tury, this first port was then expanded, and major excavation work began. At the same time, the port was equipped with an outer harbor and two wharves. At present, the port of Nice is not used for much mercantile traffic, which consists almost exclusively of trade in cement produced in the city's hinterland, but is active as a mooring place for the ferries that serve the shipping line to Corsica. On the other hand, there is an especially lively traffic of fishing boats, yachts and sailboats, especially during the summer.

Finally, various tour operators provide tourists with boats that sail from the port of Nice, offering interesting excursions along the Riviera Corniche.

View of Lympia harbor with wharves.

Photo on page 46-47:
The harbor at night.

This museum holds the largest permanent collection of works by the artist, donated to French government by Chagall himself. In the early 1970's, the architect Hermant designed this architectural work especially for the 17 paintings that comprise Chagall's Biblical Message, giving them the finest setting possible. Done over a thirteen year period from 1954 to 1967, the large paintings portray various Biblical themes, from the Creation to Noah's Ark to the Song of Songs. The national museum also displays numerous preparatory sketches for the Biblical Message, the splendid windows on the theme of Genesis, about a hundred etchings and woodcuts used to illustrate an edition of the Bible, and various other works by the great master.

1) The museum garden.
2) Marc Chagall: Elijah on the Flaming Chariot. Mosaic.

Photos by Patrick Gerin

1

The hill of Cimiez, where the ancient arena stands, is still utilized even today, especially during the spring and summer, for exhibits and shows related to the tradition and folklore of the city of Nice, including the picturesque Squash Festival in April, the May Festival, the International Folklore Festival and the famous Jazz Festival, which each July features world-renowned artists. In the arena, an amphitheater with an elliptical floor plan of which little remains, gladiators battled before crowds of no more than 4000 people, a limited capacity due to the size of the edifice, which was rather small compared with others of the period. Similar to other ancient arenas, when the weather was bad the construction could be covered by an awning or special covering cloth, as can be seen by the anchoring points for the great supporting poles, still visible today.

Next to the amphitheater on the hill of Cimiez, is an important testimony to the city's history - the Gallo-Roman archeological site, where excavations have revealed the thermal baths of ancient Cemenelum. In addition to the magnificent northern baths, used by the upper classes, there were also the eastern baths, originally reserved for women and then transformed into a Christian cathedral in the early Christian epoch (5th century AD). The baptistery is particularly interesting.

2

1

3

Pages 50-51
1) View of the Arena.
2-3) View of the thermal bath complex.

Page 52
1-2) Details of the thermal baths.
3-4) Details of the Arena.

Photos on page 53:
1) Aerial view of the Cimiez monastery.
2) Aerial view of the Cimiez Arena.

1

2

1

Adjacent to the Gallic-Roman archaeological site and the Musée Matisse, the museum primarily contains materials discovered in excavations in Cimiez or found in areas near the city. On the ground floor, there are ceramics and bronzes from the Greek and Etruscan eras and the African colonies of Rome; many have come from shipwrecks found along the coast of Nice. Of particular note is the famous mask of Silenus, with its exquisite make. The same floor holds relics of indigenous tribes dating back to the Bronze Age, as well as various objects from the Roman era. The basement floor is entirely dedicated to burial customs, with evidence of various types of burial customs used in ancient Cimiez. The collection of early Christian remains is also interesting.

1) Dancing faun from the 1st century BC.
2) Statue of Antoinette.

MUSÉE MATISSE

This museum is located in the spectacular Villa des Arènes, built on Cimiez in 1670, partially remodeled in the 19th century and finally rebuilt in the early 20th century to house a large part of the museum's works by Matisse, an auditorium and an art study center. In addition to the splendid paintings, which show the artistic life of Matisse from his beginnings to maturity (the museum also includes Flowers and Fruit, the artist's last work before he died at Cimiez in 1954), the museum's galleries display numerous drawings, engravings, the tapestry Polynesia and over fifty bronze sculptures, including the famous series of Nudes. Another section is dedicated to designs for the Chapelle du Rosaire in Vence.

1-2-3-4) Gallery exhibiting the works of Matisse.
5) Facade of the Matisse Museum.

MONASTERY

The monastery complex built around the church of Notre-Dame-de-l'Assomption is also located on the hill of Cimiez, near the Gallo-Roman archaeological site. In the 9th century, Benedictine monks built a church and convent building on the site. In the 16th century, the complex was transferred to the Franciscan order, which not only restored and expanded the original church, but also enriched it with important works of art, including three masterpieces by Ludovico Brea, who may have been the most important of the primitive painters from Nice. Completed between the late 15th and early 16th centuries, the Pietà (to the immediate left of the entry), the Crucifixion (to the left of the choir) and the Deposition (in the third chapel to the right), are the true treasures of Notre-Dame-de-l'Assomption, which also holds other works of significant artistic value, including the 17th century wooden stalls in the choir, reserved for the monks. More works of art can be seen in the nearby Franciscan museum.

The actual convent, which is closed to the public, consists of buildings overlooking two cloisters, the smallest of which, with its elegant forms, dates back to the 16th century. The larger cloister, which in the summer hosts a number of concerts, adjoins the beautiful monastery gardens, which provide a magnificent panorama of the city. The Notre-Dame-de-l'Assomption complex stands behind the Place du Monastère, with a splendid 15th century Calvary adorning the center. Near the square is the Cimiez cemetery, where a number of famous persons are buried, including Henri Matisse.

1) *View of the convent and church of Cimiez.*
2) *The Gairaut waterfall.*

CASCADE DE GAIRAUT

One of the most pleasant excursions into the nearby Nice hinterland follows a short route to the Cascade de Gairaut. This spectacular waterfall forms where the waters of the Vésubie canal (which supplies water for Nice's aqueduct) drop down two levels to flow into a small natural pool. From the nearby chapel, there is an excellent view of the city below.

Going beyond the Cascade de Gairaut, the road leads to the picturesque town of Aspremont, perched on the slops of the hill opposite Mont Chauve. The foothills of the Alps near Nice are an extremely interesting natural area, where harsh, bare landscapes blend with verdant valleys traversed by luxuriant waterways.

Nice's astronomical observatory can be reached by following the scenic route that runs east from the city. The massive square stone edifice by La Turbie was built in 1881, based on a design by Charles Garnier and funded by the patron Bischoffen. The engineer Gustave Eiffel, creator of the famous Tower of Eiffel in Paris, was in charge of the observatory's gigantic steel-covered cupola, within which is the so-called grand équatorial, the astronomical lunette that, with an astronomical diameter of 76 meters, was at the time of its construction the largest in the world. The Mont Gros center is internationally renowned in the field of astronomical research.

1) General view.
2) The great Cupola.
3) The astronomical lunette.

- 6D: Russian Orthodox Cathedral of St-Nicolas

- 5E: The railway station

- 6F: Musée Masséna

- 4F: Musée Marc Chagall

- 2G Musée Matisse Musée archéologique

- 7H: The Castle of Nice The port of Nice

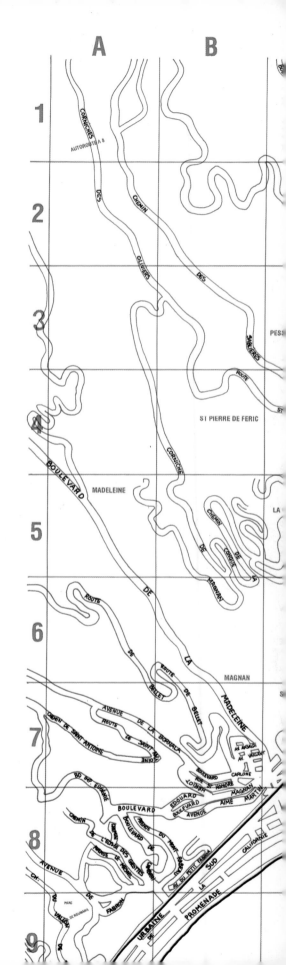